To Andrej
with love
from Mum
Christmas 1979

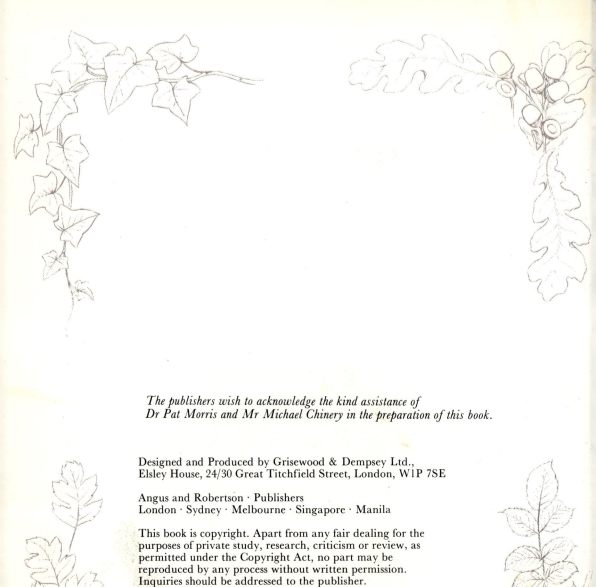

The publishers wish to acknowledge the kind assistance of
Dr Pat Morris and Mr Michael Chinery in the preparation of this book.

Designed and Produced by Grisewood & Dempsey Ltd.,
Elsley House, 24/30 Great Titchfield Street, London, W1P 7SE

Angus and Robertson · Publishers
London · Sydney · Melbourne · Singapore · Manila

First published by Angus and Robertson (U.K.) Ltd.
2 Fisher Street, London, WC1R 4QA
ISBN 0 207 95710 X

Printed and Bound by W. S. Cowell Ltd., Butter Market, Ipswich

The Squirrel

By Angela Sheehan
Illustrated by Maurice Pledger

ANGUS & ROBERTSON · PUBLISHERS

Everything was silent. The squirrel made no noise as she pushed her way out of the warm drey where she slept. It was morning and the sun was glinting on the snow. As she moved through the tree, a soft sprinkling of snow fell from the branches, but everything else was still.

It seemed that she was all alone. Dropping to the ground, the squirrel moved quickly over the snow. Her light tread left a trail of footprints in the crisp, white surface.

The squirrel shivered as the wind ruffled her fur. Scratching the hard ground with her claws, she dug into the soil, first in one spot then another. There must be some nuts somewhere.

Near the oak tree the snow was not quite so thick and the ground was softer. Here at last she found a buried acorn. Quickly she picked it up in her paws and took it to her favourite place – the stump of a horse chestnut tree. Once there, she bit hungrily into the cold, hard nut.

The squirrel spent almost the whole day eating the seeds from pine cones and sniffing about for hidden nuts and berries. Occasionally she saw a group of blackbirds searching for scraps of food on the frozen ground and a robin sheltering in the trees. The birds too were shivering in the harsh wind, but their fluffed-up feathers helped to keep them warm.

As the weak winter sun went down, the wind dropped and the showers of snow turned to icy rain. Now the squirrel was both cold and wet. It was time to go back to her drey. High in the tree she would be warm and snug for a few days and safe from the fox that prowled about at night.

The winter dragged on for several more weeks, and the squirrel was tired of winter. For months she had eaten little but pine seeds and a few acorns which she had managed to dig up. Some days had even been too cold and wet for her to leave the drey. But now spring was here and every day the weather grew milder. Every day there were more new things to eat.

Buds were swelling on the trees, and beneath them green saplings were springing up, their shoots stiff and juicy. The squirrel ripped away the bark with her strong claws and sucked up the sweet sap.

High in a nearby pine tree, the squirrel found a deserted crow's nest. With moss, twigs and strips of bark torn from the branches she soon turned the old nest into a fine new drey. The walls were tightly packed with pine needles. To get into the ball-shaped drey, the squirrel had to make a hole in the side. She covered the entrance again as soon as she was safely inside.

Although the squirrel could not be seen inside her tree-top shelter, another squirrel knew that she was there. He had a drey in another pine tree just across the clearing, and he had been watching her while she worked.

The next day the male squirrel watched the
female again as she squeezed out of the drey and
ate a breakfast of pine seeds. As she ripped off the
scales, another male squirrel that lived in a nearby
tree crept towards the horse chestnut stump and
danced around her. The female watched his fine
bushy tail and listened to his growls – but not
for long. For the first squirrel bounded to the
ground and chased the intruder away. He had seen
the female first and she was to be his mate.

Once the rival had gone, the male squirrel
turned back to the female. But she was nowhere
to be seen. She had fled back to her tree. The
male squirrel sensed where she was, scurried up
the tree trunk and bounded along branch after
branch to reach her.

Just as he was getting tired, he saw her
peeping out from behind a bunch of pine cones. He
ran as fast as he could towards her but with a
flying leap she jumped to another tree. From tree
to tree he chased her until she too was tired. They
were both far from home when she stopped and let
him come close to her. He clutched her warm soft
fur and they mated.

As the weeks went by the female's body grew fat. Inside her, three tiny squirrel kittens were growing and it would soon be time for them to be born. The squirrel needed a warm drey where she could have her babies and bring them up.

One day when she was looking for food the squirrel caught sight of a hole in the trunk of an oak tree. Sniffing the air, she pushed her whiskers into the dark hollow. As she did so, a terrified starling flew out of the darkness – leaving behind her three new-laid eggs.

What luck! The squirrel loved birds' eggs of any kind. Picking them up, she carried them, one by one, along a branch, broke their shells, and licked up the warm yolks.

The squirrel had not only found herself a
tasty meal in the oak tree. She had found the
perfect place for a nursery. Building on to the
starling's nest, she added more leaves, mosses and
twigs to make a drey inside the hole. The floor of
the drey would not be soft enough for the babies,
so she pulled tufts of fur from her belly to line the
nest. Her kittens were born next day and they had a
fine bed of fur to sleep on.

The new-born kittens were as tiny as mice and their hairless bodies were bright pink. It was ten days before they were able to see, and by then their fur had grown.

The kittens slept for most of the time and sucked milk from their mother. Sometimes when they were sound asleep and safely snuggled up together their mother left them to find food for herself. But she never went away for long.

Within about seven weeks, the kittens were almost fully grown and there was hardly enough room for all of them in the drey. Their mother, who now had a fine new summer coat, brought them young pine shoots to eat. Often they peeped out of the hole to see the world and sometimes they ran out and played among the branches. One of them was even brave enough to go all the way down to the ground. But he did not go very far.

His mother knew how dangerous it was on the ground and tried to pick him up in her mouth. But he was so heavy that she almost could not carry him.

As soon as the squirrels were strong enough
to find food for themselves they went farther and
farther from the drey. One even tried to build a
new drey for himself.

He gathered twigs in his mouth and carried
them to the fork of a pine tree. Some of them
slipped to the ground, so he went back for more.
He gathered leaves from the ground and carried
them up the trunk, too. He was so busy with his
new game that he did not notice the dark pine
marten ready to leap on him from the next branch.

As the animal pounced the squirrel sprang
away. He felt his tail slip through the marten's
claws. Not looking round, the frightened squirrel
ran for his life. Leaping from branch to branch
and tree to tree, he could feel and hear the branches
crashing as the pine marten came closer and closer.
His legs ached and his teeth chattered. With a last
desperate lunge he made the biggest jump of his life.

He seemed almost to fly. Stretching his
paws, he just managed to clutch the end of a clump
of leaves. But the thin branch bent under his weight
and sprang up and down. The ground was far, far
beneath him. Terrified, the squirrel clung to the
swaying branch and then gently drew himself along
it to safety.

The marten bared his teeth as he watched
the squirrel from the other side of the gap. Even if
he managed to leap the gap, he knew that the
branch would not hold him.

Weak and out of breath, the squirrel rested
on a branch. At last he was safe, but he was so far
from home that he could never go back. Now he
really would have to build a drey for himself.

As the summer passed, the squirrels ate more and more. Stripping the scales from cones and the bark from trees was easy, but cracking nuts was much more difficult.

When their mother found a hazel nut she gnawed a neat hole in the top and then split the hard shell with just one bite. But the young ones had to gnaw and gnaw to get at the sweet kernels inside the nuts. It would take lots of practice before they could split the shells cleanly in two like their mother.

There were now so many nuts and berries
about that the squirrels could not possibly eat them
all. So they buried some of them. Picking them up
one by one they dug a little hole for each and
popped the nut or berry into it. Each hole was
covered by leaves and soil.

The wood mice also buried nuts, although
they usually came out only at night. They often
buried lots of nuts together in one hole. Sometimes
in winter the squirrels found one of these larders.
Then they had a real feast.

The best hazel tree of all was far from the
other trees in the wood. It stood in a hedgerow on
the other side of the stream and the squirrels had
to swim to reach it. The mother squirrel went there
one evening. She swam across the stream and spent
some time feasting on toadstools and nuts that
lay by its roots. She did not know that one of her
young squirrels had followed her.

He had never swum before and it took him a
long time to cross the stream. It was nearly dark
when he reached the tree and his mother had
already set off back to her drey. He was all alone
and a cold wind was blowing.

The young squirrel shivered by the foot of
the hedgerow. He looked up at the big grey
branches of an ash tree, knowing that it would be
safer to climb up to the top and stay there for the
night. But first he would have just one hazel nut.

He hopped a little way but as he stretched
out his paws, a huge tawny owl swooped silently out
of the tree. Its great wings spread over the helpless
squirrel and its talons sank through his fur. The
squirrel would never eat the nut and never return
to the oak tree where he was born.

As the weather grew colder and colder, the squirrels grew thick winter coats. The mother squirrel built yet another drey. All her young squirrels had gone now. The young female she had reared had built several dreys during the summer and, like her mother, was ready to build a really strong one for the winter. She lived in a beautiful spruce tree. Next spring she would find a mate and bring up her own family.

The squirrels had eaten so many acorns and other fruits that they were quite fat. Their winter

dreys were soon built. There seemed to be dreys in all the trees. Many of the other squirrels had had another family in the autumn and there were lots of young squirrels in the woods.

The oaks, beeches and hawthorns dropped their last browning leaves, making a thick carpet on the ground. Their leafless branches looked cold and stark against the warm green conifers where the squirrels built their nests. But beneath the leaves there was a rich store of nuts – if only the squirrels could find them.

More About Squirrels

Where Squirrels Live
There are more than 300 different kinds of squirrels in the world. The red squirrels in the story live in Europe, mostly in coniferous forests. They spend most of their time in the trees and only come down to the ground to look for food.

Claws for Climbing
Squirrels are very good climbers. The sharp claws on their paws keep them from slipping as they run and jump among the branches high above the ground. As it leaps, the squirrel stretches out its four legs and uses its flattened, bushy tail to steer and balance. When squirrels drop to the ground to escape from danger, their tails act like parachutes to slow their fall.

Food for all Seasons
Although red squirrels sometimes eat the eggs and nestlings of birds, nearly all the rest of their food comes from plants. In the pine forests there are plenty of pine seeds to eat all the year round. In other forests there are nuts and acorns to eat too.

In spring the squirrels eat the new buds and gnaw the bark away from young trees to get at the sap. In summer there are berries and soft fruits. In autumn there are nuts and seeds and plenty of toadstools.

When the squirrels have eaten their fill, they usually bury some nuts and berries. The cold earth acts like a deep-freeze and keeps them fresh throughout the winter. The squirrels bury each nut separately. Once they have covered the holes they cannot remember where the nuts are. Finding them again is probably a matter of luck and a good sense of smell.

front teeth

A squirrel gnawing a pine cone

Nutcrackers
If you watch a young squirrel eating a nut, you will see how long it takes to gnaw through the shell. Watch an adult squirrel and you will see how quickly it pierces the shell and splits it clean in two. The young squirrels have to learn how to split nuts by watching the adults. It takes a lot of practice before they too become expert nutcrackers.

When they are not cracking nuts, gnawing bark or ripping the seeds from pine cones, squirrels are always grinding their teeth. This is because their four front teeth never stop growing. The squirrels have to keep grinding and gnawing to stop their teeth becoming too long.

nut split by adult

nuts gnawed by young

How squirrels crack nuts

A squirrel's tracks

Looking for Squirrels

Squirrels are very hard to see in the woods but there are many signs that will tell you where to look for them. First there are their dreys which are high in the trees in winter and lower during the summer.

On the ground you may see their footprints and these tracks may lead you to a squirrel's 'breakfast table' – a favourite tree stump where the squirrel eats its food. Around it you will see the remains of pine cones, acorns and nut shells.

Look at the nearby trees and you may see places where the squirrels have ripped away the bark to reach the sap or gnawed it with their teeth. And in spring look at the saplings to see if the squirrels have bitten off their new buds.

Grey Cousins

The red squirrel has always lived in Europe but its cousin the grey squirrel, which used to live only in America, now lives here too. Apart from its colour the grey squirrel is almost the same as the red squirrel. But it is much bolder and does a lot of damage to the countryside. There are now so many grey squirrels that farmers and foresters think of them as pests. They eat their food crops and kill whole trees by stripping too much bark from them.

Hiding from Danger

Red squirrels are timid creatures with few enemies, but even so they are always alert for danger. In the trees their most dangerous enemy is the pine marten which can move as fast and jump as far as they can. When a pine marten is about the squirrels hide behind leaves and cones and stay so still that they cannot be seen. On the ground, where foxes and wildcats prowl, even the slightest noise will send a squirrel scurrying up the nearest tree. Other enemies that squirrels have to watch out for are birds of prey, such as owls and eagles.

A grey squirrel